Cognitive Behavioral Therapy

A 100% Chemical-Free Approach to
Eliminate Anxiety, Depression, and
Intrusive Thoughts And Start Feeling Good
About Life

Nick Anderson

Table of Contents:

Introduction

Phobias. Depression. Anxiety. Post-traumatic stress. Well, there's been a massive shift in the world of psychiatry to finding biological bases for these conditions (and their matching chemical therapies). It appears that we've reached a point where treatment emphasis focuses too heavily on medication.

The truth? While many people are helped by pharmaceutical products, there are many others who simply can't tolerate such medication. What happens to these people? What kind of options do they have? On top of that in addition to these individuals, there are also other people who just don't want to try any kind of meditation at all.

What about them? Is there any treatment available for them? This is where cognitive behavioral therapy (or 'CBT') comes in. Cognitive behavioral therapy works with the way the human mind processes stimuli and perceived reality. By retraining the mind to handle certain memories and stimuli a certain way, people can be taught to handle post-traumatic stress, anxiety, depression, and phobias better.

There are two ways to do CBT: psychiatrist or psychologist mediated and supervised and personal CBT. Personal CBT involves adopting a thinking technique that is based on our personal terms and on our schedule. This is not professionally mediated and supervised.

CBT as a whole enables us to separate our feelings from our thoughts, live lives in perspective, focus on the big picture, keep our eyes on the things that truly matter, maintain balance, and control stress. In other words, with proper CBT training, we would be able to train our minds to work for us instead of against us.

Left undisciplined, it's very easy for our minds to adopt negative mental habits which can produce a lot of unnecessary stress, tension, and negative coping behaviors. These can lead to low self-esteem, lack of self-confidence, damaged or strained relationships, and lower life success. The bottom line is quite simple and straightforward: cognitive behavioral therapy enables people to live fuller lives by controlling how their mind works.

Chapter 1: The Root Of Unnecessary Stress And Depression

It's easy to think that depression and stress are automatic. It's tempting to believe that once you start feeling stressed or you start feeling down, there's really nothing you can do about it. It just takes a life of its own and you are going to be in for one hell of a ride. We feel that when a certain thought or trigger enters our minds, we really can't control our emotions. Soon enough, we start reacting in a negative way.

These range of negative emotions don't just stay in our heads. Sooner or later, we find ourselves saying negative things and doing negative things. What makes this so frustrating is the fact that we do this repeatedly despite the following. First, we know better. After all, we've seen this happen before.

Maybe the thought of your ex-boyfriend cheating on you triggers you to overeat or to lash out by treating your current boyfriend badly. You know what happens. You can see the pattern. You know better but you keep repeating the pattern over and over again. Next, we end up in this negative cycle of thoughts and actions despite the fact that we know the end result is bad.

We've seen it before. We know the bad effects. We know what happens when we start detecting these very negative emotions. But we sit back and let it happen. We know what's going to happen. We let it play out anyway. It's as if you are watching a movie of your life. It feels that there's really nothing you can do except to stay in the seat and just watch the movie play out.

You want to turn your head but you can't help but look at the screen. At the back of your mind, you're hoping against hope that somehow someway the ending this time will be different. But you know better. We end up with this negative pattern of thoughts, language, and actions despite the fact that we hate the bad effects. It's not enough that we know that there will be bad effects. We hate the effects. It's not like you want these things to happen. Still, despite the fact that you know that this will end badly and that you hate what this does to your life, you do it anyway.

Finally, we remain trapped in this cycle despite the fact that other people are telling us that this is a bad thing. It's not like this is subjective. It's not like you're just seeing this from a negative perspective. This is objectively bad.

Other people are telling you to your face. They're not hiding it from you. They're not whispering behind your back. They are telling you in no uncertain terms. Maybe they say it out of concern. Maybe your friends want to help you. Or maybe people just want you to cut it out. Whatever their motivations may be, this negative chain reaction that you're feeling and acting out is an objective problem.

You Are On An Emotional Rollercoaster

The root of this issue really boils down to the fact that you are on an emotional rollercoaster. Every single day, your senses detect thousands of stimuli from the outside world. The way your mind is set up or trained filters these stimuli. You have to understand that these stimuli apply to people around you. You're all picking up the same signals.

But the effect on you is going to be different because of the way your mind turns the stimuli into thoughts. Your perception of these stimuli is the first step in the emotional rollercoaster that you're riding. This is the first stage in the emotional rollercoaster you're riding. You analyze or read the things that you choose to be aware of. As the old saying goes, there are always two sides to the story.

Well, given how chaotic and complicated life is, there are at least two sides to the story. There's probably more. There's usually more. Regardless, if you are caught in an emotional rollercoaster, you read your thoughts a certain way. These interpretations don't stay in your mind. They impact your emotions. They're not emotionally neutral.

And these emotions that you get trigger words. Now, there are certain words that are going to make the situation worse. You know that. There are also other words that can diffuse the situation. Eventually, this translates to actions. Believe it or not, the world only pays attention. Once your emotional rollercoaster reaches the words or action stage, all of us are entitled to our own thoughts, analysis, and reading of our thoughts.

All of us are entitled to our emotions. But once we express what we're feeling inside in the form of words or actions that's when the world sits up and pays attention. At that point, we start changing our world. That's the point where we create results or lack thereof. What makes it all frustrating is that it seems like you can't stop the rollercoaster.

It just feels like the moment you start thinking of that abuse that happened in your childhood or the fact that the rent is coming due and you have no money in your pocket or bank account triggers this wave of negative emotions which leads to the same repetitive negative actions. You are really powerless against this because you keep seeing the same pattern play out again and again. It's easy to understand why you'd feel that you can't stop the rollercoaster.

But the truth is you can. How can I be so sure? Well, look at the chain that starts with the stimuli which of course you can't control. But once you choose to perceive the stimuli that's the point when you are in control. There's a point in time when you are in control. That's the point in the process when you are in control. You can control your thoughts. You can control your analysis of what you choose to think about. You can definitely control what you read into what you choose to perceive. After this point, it becomes harder and harder to control things seriously because once you get emotional, it's going to be very hard to stop the rollercoaster in its tracks. Your emotional habits just kick in and then the words start flying out and you start engaging in the same predictable negative behavior pattern.

CBT is all about helping you maximize your ownership and control of the emotional roller coaster process range starting with thought formation proceeding to analysis and reading all the way to emotional response. That's how you stop the roller coaster and CBT enables you to do that. The way you perceive stimuli has a pronounced impact on how you perform. In a 1990

University of Pennsylvania study conducted by Richard L. Metzger reported in the Journal of Clinical Psychology, study participants were split up between two people and tested to sort materials into two categories.

Prior to the sorting action, participants were surveyed whether they were worried about the task or not. Subjects were surveyed whether they worry 50 percent of the time or more or less than 50 percent of the time. The people who said that they worry more than half the time showed a significant disruption in their ability to sort objects as the sorting task's difficulty level increased.

Following up on these subjects, the researchers were able to demonstrate that the disruption in the performance of the test subjects was correlated and was directly produced by the level of negative thoughts they had. The study conclusively proves that our thoughts have a direct impact on our actions. Similarly, negative thought patterns can lead to habitual personal actions that can have physical or medical consequences.

In a study out of the University of Pittsburgh which was published in The Journal Circulation in 2009, a team led by Hilary A. Tindle looked at research data on almost 100,000 women and cross-referenced 100,000 women and found that the most cynical study subjects developed heart disease at a much higher rate than the least cynical subjects. In fact, the cynical women who are also pessimistic had a much higher chance of dying over the time-frame of the study.

This is in comparison with those who viewed humanity with a higher level of optimism. Finally, in a study out of the University of Minnesota led by Susan A. Everson-Rose published in The Journal of Stroke, the 2014 study showed that people who are hostile or unfriendly and had exhibited chronic depressive symptoms and stress faced higher stroke risks than patients who were objectively kinder and friendlier. Again, emotional states lead to certain actions which produce certain results.

Chapter 2: What CBT is and what it isn't?

Given how central CBT is to changing behavior, it's very important to point what it is and what it isn't. A lot of people are under the impression that CBT is something that is produced through pharmaceutical assisted therapy. That can be the case, but CBT, ideally, should be implemented alone. CBT in of itself has the following qualities.

It is 100% chemical-free

Thanks to the popularity of drugs like Prozac and Celexa, a large percentage of people suffering from depression and anxiety disorders in the United States use pharmaceutical products to control their systems. Paired with the right counseling, such treatment can lead to long-term positive results.

There has been a sea-change in how psychiatric and psychological, as well as emotional coping issues are dealt with in the United States and elsewhere. Previously, there was a lot of emphasis on talk therapy. Thanks to rise of psychological pharmaceutical products, there has been a shift to medication.

The problem here is the fact that not everybody responds well to these chemical compounds. In fact, a significant percentage of people who take antidepressants or anti-anxiety medication do not show any improvement. On top of that, there are people who are worried about the long-term effects and consequences of these medications.

Make no mistake, even the current wave of SSRI medications which focus on the brain's Serotonin levels for therapy has some very strong side effects. You lose your sexual drive. Men can suffer from erectile dysfunction. There have also been reports of drowsiness, diarrhea, insomnia and dizziness.

Ironically, people who suffer from anxiety disorders who use Serotonin-based therapies report nervousness, restlessness or agitation. There is a need for a chemical-free alternative and CBT delivers that.

Focus on mental processes

CBT teaches you how to focus on your mental processes. For lack of a better word, it teaches you how to own these processes. Instead of just sitting back and thinking that your negative thoughts are simply just going to progress into negative actions without any control on your part, you learn how to take control of the process. Either you learn how to reduce its negative effects or turn what would otherwise have been a negative result into something positive. You feel more in control.

Focus on mental associations, beliefs, feeling and behaviors

When you practice CBT, you learn how your mind is currently trained. You understand that the way you think is ultimately a choice. You may not think it was a choice. You may not think that you purposefully or intentionally chose to think the way you do, but you did. At some point in the past, you picked up certain mental and emotional habits.

The key behind CBT is to become aware of these mental associations. You open your eyes to how you connect certain stimuli you detect from the outside world with certain mental imagery and emotional states. You also see the connection between these emotions and the actions you habitually take.

Learning skills to take control over mental processes

It's easy to say that we should just control our thoughts. This is one of those things that you can safely categorize as "easier said than done." Anybody can say this. Few are the people who can actually pull it off. With CBT, you join the ranks of the few because you learn specific skills for controlling your mental processes.

You don't just focus on theory. You don't focus on what you should be doing. CBT actually steps you through the process of actively taking control over these processes.

Fully conscious process

In the past, there were therapy regimens that focused on hypnosis or any other type of behavioral control where the subject is not really in control. Basically, people are trained to focus on an object and then they would be "reprogrammed" to think or behave a certain way. There are other therapy systems that involved dreamlike states, so that the person would passively absorb certain suggestions that would change their behavior.

CBT doesn't involve any of these. This is a fully conscious process. You are fully aware of what is going on and you have full choice. Nobody is tricking you into thinking in a way that you normally don't. You are also trained to focus on each and every thought. This is the complete opposite of subliminal, subconscious or other types of therapy.

Fully logical process while taking emotions and feelings into account

Last but least, CBT is rooted in logic. It is rooted in reason. While your feelings and emotions are important, it uses basic logic to help you take control over your mental and emotional processes. They key to CBT is to actually master your emotional state.

A lot of our negative mental habits take the form of our emotions getting the better of us. CBT enables us to overcome this.

What CBT isn't

There are many misconceptions about CBT like its formal definition. These cannot be further from the truth. Here is just a short list of the wild and wacky ideas that are often passed off as CBT or confused with it.

Hypnosis

Wouldn't it be great if somebody just flashed a light in your eyes or swung some sort of watch in front of you and you fall into a trance and when the hypnotist snaps his or her fingers, your problems magically disappear? This situation is very tempting. Who wouldn't want a quick, cheap and effective way to get out from under our emotional and psychological habits? Who wouldn't want to just wave a wand and kiss all our negative behavioral patterns goodbye?

Unfortunately, hypnosis is not CBT. There are a lot of people who vouch for the effectiveness of hypnosis, but the results they get are probably due to something else. Hypnosis claims that you can reprogram your mind through some sort of outside assistance. This reprogramming is based on the outside intervention using some form of physical analog.

It may well turn out that whatever results hypnosis brings to the table is due to the human mind's susceptibility to suggestion. But please understand, just like the placebo effect, this doesn't apply to everybody. Some people respond really well to placebos, most don't. That's why we need medication.

The same applies to hypnosis. Some people may respond favorably to hypnosis, but most people do not. That's why therapy like CBT exists. Hypnosis also requires people to enter a less than fully aware or fully conscious state. This is a huge contrast from how CBT works. CBT requires that you are fully aware of your surroundings and your mental state, and you're fully conscious.

Hypnosis supposedly gets its power from the subconscious. Unfortunately, one of the most debunked and discredited areas of psychology, involves the Freudian ideas of the subconscious. We're getting into quite a murky territory here. In contrast, CBT is based on pure rationality, and there are strong signs to back up its key claims.

Wishful thinking

Another body of practice that CBT is often associated with or confused for being is wishful thinking. The idea is that if you keep wishing, it triggers some sort of change within you that sooner or later, that wish will be fulfilled. According to this thinking, you just have to wish repeatedly, clearly, consciously and that alternate reality that you thought was so impossible and so out of reach will become true soon enough.

The idea behind wishful thinking is actually more rational than it seems. While it's still largely false and ineffective, the idea behind it is that when wishing to enter a different mindset, things become possible. You should then use this emotional break from your normal reality to motivate you to break free from it completely.

The problem with this thinking is that people who engage in wishful thinking don't use it as a solution. It's really a form of daydreaming. You know that you are in a harsh relationship. You know that your partner doesn't respect you or treat you the right way. Maybe you're abusing that person, or they are abusing you. Maybe you know that you're stuck at your job or your business. Maybe you know that you have certain bad habits or addictions.

But instead of using wishful thinking to solve these dilemmas by making hard decisions, people take the other route. What do they do? They look for an escape. It's not uncommon for people in abusive relationships to imagine themselves in perfect relationships. It's as if their lives have been turned into some soap opera.

It's not uncommon for people who are suffering from memories of abusive childhoods to imagine grand futures for themselves. Granted, that there is a significant emotional benefit to this. After all, thinking this way lessens the pain. It enables you to dull the trauma. But the problem is, it's like taking drugs. You get too numb, and instead of waking you up like a nice jolt of caffeine, you get used to the sedative effect of your fantasies.

They mentally and emotionally dull, or they drag you from taking the hard steps you need to take. People who are being beaten by their partners often engage in this. The wishful thinking is that he or she is a great person, they don't really mean it, and they will get their act together soon enough. Wishful thinking can work, but you can't use it as a drug. You can't use to it dumb yourself from making hard decisions today.

Wish fulfillment

CBT is not wish fulfillment. Wish fulfillment involves focusing on a wish or alternate reality and seeing the things that are happening in your life fall into place with that alternate reality. In other words, it's imagining things that aren't there. Now, there are certain effective elements of wish fulfillment that can give people the motivation and drive they need to truly change their mental habits and, by extension, change their lives.

The problem is, with wish fulfillment, the focus is primarily on emotional payoffs right now. Think if it this way. You know that you are in a dead-end job. You know full well that despite how many years you've put in, you're just not going to get the kind of career fulfillment you're looking for. It's just not going to happen.

So, you look at what's going on and you imagine that this is the very best you can achieve, and you draw a lot of happiness from this artificial reality that you've set up for yourself. You trick yourself into thinking that this is the best you can do, and you are actually quite happy. The problem with this is that it's ultimately self-deception.

You're not really working towards your ultimate wishes because those involve some sort of breakthrough. Instead, you're giving yourself excuses to settle for what you have. Deep down inside, you don't really want to take the necessary and often inconvenient and uncomfortable steps to get the rewards that you know you could achieve, so you play these mind games.

CBT doesn't work this way. It works with the reality of your life and changes your internal processing mechanisms so you can direct them towards outcomes you have specifically chosen. Everything is well drawn out. You're not chasing after a feeling You're not making excuses for yourself. You're not giving yourself a fancy back story so you don't have to try as hard.

CBT is rooted in reality and also pushes you towards a higher standard because it is not based on playing games with yourself just so you could settle for your personal misery.

The Law Of Attraction

The law of attraction states that if you are so focused on some sort of alternate version of your reality, sooner or later your world starts realigning itself around that alternative reality that is locked in your mind. Believe it or not, there is a lot of truth to the law of attraction. Unfortunately, the way most people carry out the law leaves much to be desired. They end up practicing wishful thinking or some version of wish fulfillment.

The idea behind the law of attraction is to let your ideal vision change you. This is the part that most people do not want to get. They can get it because it's spelled out, but they don't want to get it. Why? It takes work and it's scary. After all, change is scary. Ideally, the law of attraction is all about focusing on the thing that you want to attract and letting it change your emotional state to the point that you bear action.

It is actually you who bring that reality to life because you are able to be at the right place at the right time, doing the right things that produce the right outcomes. In other words, the law of attraction requires intentionality. A part of this is the willingness to take intentional action. They do go hand in hand. Unfortunately, a lot of people who are naturally drawn to the law of attraction discount that part. They just focus on the intentional thoughts part. That's right, they focus on the easy part. Well, the funny thing about the law of attraction is if you truly believe in it, everything does become easy because the more passionate you are about your grand vision or your specific objective, the more things will fall into place.

You get the energy to do what you need to do. You get the personal power you need to overcome your fears, your pride, or your past negative memories to do what you need to do. Ultimately, it all turns on the actions that the law of attraction frees you to do. Most people don't see that part. In fact, there are tons of law of attraction books out there that simply just pay lip service to that part even though that part is the most important one.

You can be as focused on your alternative reality as much as possible. But if you don't let the energy that that focus creates, flow to the rest of your life, you're going to be stuck where you are. CBT has some similarity to this in the sense that you have to believe the system. When you believe that taking control over your mental processes can have an effect on your emotions and your decisions and habitual actions, this leads you to a state of internal mental flow.

Things become possible again. You have the energy you need to pick apart your emotional puzzles. You get the power you need to overcome your normal tendency to do things a certain way once you are triggered by external stimuli. In short, the law of attraction and CBT both have the idea of mental focus in common.

However, with CBT, your feet never leave the ground. Everything is practical. You just need to follow the steps and repeat it consistently to enjoy significant results. With the law of attraction, if you apply it in a very imbalanced way by just dwelling so much on the focus part, the rest of the equation may not become a reality and benefit you.

What do all these CBT alternatives have in common?

There are all theoretical or speculative. While there are some glimmers of scientific fact in running though their threads, taken as whole, they are speculative at best and scams at worst. CBT is rooted in clinical science. In fact, the latest evidence of this was a 2012 study out of the University of

Arizona led by a researcher, Sarah Hamill-Skoch.

Her study showed that adolescents who went through CBT therapy can overcome mental health issues, mood disorders and depression. Similarly, in a 2005 University of Pennsylvania study lead by Andrew C. Butlera, they found that CBT compares favorably to antidepressants when it comes to handling depression. Butlera's findings were published in the Science Direct journal.

Finally, in a 2008 study out of the University of Pennsylvania, CBT is shown to at least be as effective as antidepressant chemicals when treating patients who suffer from major depression. Published by Robert J. Derubeis, the researchers found that CBT also offers promise when it comes to treating anxiety and is especially effective when patients are observed over the long term. This team's findings were published in PubMed.

Chapter 3: A Quick History of Cognitive Behavioral Therapy

CBT traces its origin from the work of Dr. Aaron T. Beck. Originally, he was focusing on depression and if there was a better therapy for this often debilitating condition.

His work took many twists and turns and he became really curious about the connection between people's ability to associate things with experiences or concepts in their minds with emotional states. This is called associative thinking.

As he did his research, he found out that there was an important link between positivity and associative thinking. It turns out that when we associate certain memories with certain emotional states, we actually have a lot of control over the process.

Most people would think that if you had a bad experience, there is really only one way to remember that experience. If you feel sad, fearful, angry, upset or guilty, the thinking was that these were the only emotional readings or interpretations you can have about your experience.

Dr. Beck's research focused on positive people. It turns out that these people had negative experiences too, but they are less likely to enter negative emotional states. If it's true that people engage in associative thinking, why is it that these people found a way to cope and get over their past trauma in a positive way?

Dr. Beck discovered an important link. How you think about something affects your mood, your emotions and how you respond. That's right. How you think about something involves your choice of interpretation or your attitude towards the thing that you're thinking about.

This is not something that is set in stone. Just because something is negative in the minds of a lot of people it doesn't necessarily mean that it should be negative in your mind. You are in charge of how you think about something.

The effect on your mood and your emotions and your actions are quite strong. But in terms of control, it turns out that people have a lot more control than they give themselves credit for at the thinking stage.

Breaking Down the Connection

Associative thinking really is a form of mental habit. For whatever reason, you have associated certain interpretations with certain stimuli. Now, this doesn't mean that everybody would have that same association.

This is where Dr. Beck's research on positive people really stood out. Just because most people would normally associate negative reactions to a certain set of stimuli, that fact alone doesn't mean that negativity is the only response.

He focused on a positive response and where that came from. And ultimately, it came down to choice. He was able to track how people end up taking the same actions when subjected to a certain stimuli.

As mentioned in an earlier part of this book, when people perceive stimuli from the outside world, they analyze it. This is your thinking process. This is where Dr. Beck focused his research on.

At this stage, people think about the stimuli they chose to perceive. This is a choice. This is not forced on you, this is not a function of your genetics, this is a choice.

It may not seem like much of a choice because you have habitually taken this choice over and over again. It might even seem automatic, but it's still a choice. At some point in the past, you have chosen to respond this way.

Maybe you have chosen this response so many times that you just have grown accustomed to it. It just feels like second nature to you, but it's still a choice. This analysis part leads to an emotional state.

Dr. Aaron Beck highlighted in his work that positive people are positive because they choose to analyze their stimuli in an empowering way. They chose to look at what's going on in a way that doesn't leave them feeling crushed, small, powerless, voiceless, and ultimately, lost.

This, of course, has a tremendous effect on people's emotional state. Depending on how you read your situation and process your thoughts, your judgments can either lead to a positive emotional state, a neutral one, or something very negative.

Past this point, of course, the train will leave the station. In other words, it's harder and harder to control your reactions past this point.

Once you have entered this negative emotional state, don't be surprised if you start saying negative things. It won't be too shocking when you engage in a negative or self-defeating coping action.

It's really hard to stop the chain reaction at this point because all the force of all that preceding habitual action proves to be just too much. You have to stop it as close to the stimuli as possible.

Take the case of a person who is going about his or her day and all of a sudden the image of that person's abusive ex-partner flashes in his or her mind. There are two ways this can play out.

Attitude #1

If this person had an attitude of hate, anger, regret or guilt about his or her ex, they probably would interpret that image or that memory of his or her time with their ex in a way that leads to either them running away from the problem and avoiding it. They'd rather not deal with. They know that it's negative and they just basically don't want to confront it.

If this is their attitude, the chance of that person getting into a relationship with another abusive partner is actually quite high. How come? They're not actually dealing with their negative memory.

They're not trying to learn from it, they're not trying to detect certain behavioral patterns, and they're not trying to make certain changes as far as their own behavior and attitude are concerned. This increases the chance that this person will end up in the same type of relationship.

Attitude #2

Alternatively, this person can have a different attitude. In this alternative scenario, this person focuses on the fact that he or she chose his or her abusive ex. They focus on their ability to choose.

They focus on the fact that they chose the wrong person in the past, but this doesn't mean that they should choose the same type of person. Instead, they realized that they have the ability to choose and that this choice is power.

They can easily choose a better person. They can choose a person that would bring out the best in them.

When you focus on your ability to choose and you focus on your need for positive results like respect, love, acceptance, nurturing and companionship, you would probably select a better person or you would work with your partner to produce better results in your relationship.

I hope you can see the difference between the two attitudes. There is really not much difference in terms of the scenario, but there is a big difference in terms of the attitude or how the other person thought about the same experience.

The stimuli is the same: the image of an abusive ex-partner flashing in the person's mind. However, depending on your attitude, you can enjoy two totally different effects. You have two totally different mood sets. You probably would be talking differently, depending on your attitude.

Obviously, somebody who is simmering in hate, anger, regret and guilt is going to probably be talking about certain things and sounding like a certain type of person. Of course, the actions the person is likely to take is going to be heavily affected depending on whether they feel empowered over their ability to choose or they just feel anger, regret, guilt and confusion.

Here's another example. Two people see a very expensive car. They're standing on a street corner and a very expensive car passes by.

The first person says, "I can't afford that. It's a very expensive car. That car is worth more than my house or my apartment. I probably would need to work ten years just to afford that car. This is unfair. The rich are getting richer, the poor are getting poorer. Poor me."

When somebody thinks this way, what do you think happens? When they say, "I cannot afford that" or "The rich are getting richer," basically, what they are saying is that there is no hope for them. How can there be hope because the person said, "I can't afford that?"

This is a statement of fact. This is a statement of limitation. When you say this statement, you are making a declaration that, based on what you know and the reality that you are living, you can't afford that car. There's no way.

Also, when people say, "That's for rich people" or "The rich people are getting richer," they're also defining themselves as poor and they are outside of the realm of possibility of earning enough money to buy the same car.

They consider themselves the "other." They don't even see themselves in the picture. It's just about the rich getting richer and the poor getting poorer.

When people go through this thought process, we focus on our judgment, and our judgment says that the reality of owning a very expensive car is simply beyond our grasp. It's just not going to happen.

Now, does this mean that people who think this way will never ever get to own such a car? Of course, not. People do get lucky. People do stumble upon certain circumstances that materially change their situation. There's always that possibility.

But in terms of probability, if you think this way, it's less likely you'll be able to change your condition. You feel trapped. You feel powerless because you said to yourself, "I cannot afford that. There's just really no way. I cannot see any action I can take right here, right now, that would lead me to afford that car."

Please understand that this is not just a statement of personal reality, but it's also self-programming. The more you repeat this, the more you reinforce this reality.

The second person saw the exact same car. However, this other person thought of a different question. He or she said, "How can I afford that car? What do I need to do to afford that car?"

When people think along these lines, they push their brain to solve problems. They tap their mind's inexhaustible ability to come up with creative, resourceful and imaginative solutions.

Even coming up with the idea of maybe coming up with some sort of new burger stand and then selling enough burgers to get enough cash to buy that car gives you a sense of optimism.

Alternatively, people might think, "Okay, I can work hard at my job and get promoted enough, make enough, invest this, and this would lead to enough cash to afford that car."

Whatever route you take, it all leads to the same place when you ask these initial questions. You always end up optimistic. At the very least, you don't feel crushed, you don't feel small, powerless and lacking control. In other words, you don't feel like the first person in our scenario.

Indeed, people who think in terms of "How can I afford that?" position themselves in such a way that any progress they achieve leading to their goal gives them a more empowered feeling. They start looking at the baby steps that they take towards their goals as stepping stones, which leads to greater and greater levels of competence and self confidence.

In other words, the more they achieve, the better they feel about themselves, and the more possible things become. It becomes some grand adventure. And sooner or later, with enough focus and consistency, they get to where they want to go.

Do you see how this works? And these individuals are exactly the same except for their thoughts. All people can choose to be Person 1 or Person 2. And it all happens in between your ears.

None of this has to do with your skin color, how tall you are, how big you are, your religion, whether your parents loved you and took care of you, how big your home is –

none of that matters. Instead, the only thing at issue is your mindset.

In a 2013 study out of the Florida State University College of Medicine, researcher Angelina Sutin found a link between how people view themselves and their actions later on in life.

Sutin studied teenagers who were of normal weight. She surveyed the test subjects and some of them said that they thought that they were overweight. Checking up on these people several years later, Sutin found that the teenagers who said that they view themselves as overweight were more likely to be obese later on in life.

This study highlights the impact of our thoughts. Negative thoughts not only affect you mentally and emotionally, they also have a physical impact. Sutin's research was published in The Sage journal.

Similarly, in a 1985 study out of Oxford University conducted by a research team led by Goodheart DE, the researcher sampled students who recently experienced a very stressful event in their life. The survey was designed to determine whether the respondents focused on the negative or positive outcomes regarding the stressful event.

Study participants who reported mostly on the negative results of a stressful life event tended to have lower self esteem, they had higher levels of psychological trauma, and they were not very satisfied with themselves. The researchers conducted two interviews: immediately after the event, and two months after the event. This study indicates the link between low self esteem and self satisfaction with what we focus on.

It also suggests that there is a self-reinforcing mechanism. If you focus mostly on the negative outcome of something that happened to you, you tend to have lower self esteem. And because you have low self esteem, you tend to focus on the negative side of whatever you experience.

And this gets the process going again. It's a self-reinforcing mechanism. It can either go up, which can lead to positive self esteem, or it can go down, which leads to worse and worse self esteem and self satisfaction.

Finally, in a 2012 study out of the University of Pennsylvania conducted by Jianghong Liu, people with low self esteem were observed in terms of aggression. This aggression took two forms: physical and verbal.

Interestingly enough, individuals with low self esteem tend to display higher risks of aggression. They're more likely to lash out at others.

Again, how we think about things impacts how we behave. And the more aggressive we become, the higher the chance that people would respond in a negative way, which leads us to feel even worse about ourselves. When we feel bad about ourselves, we are more likely to lash out in a negative way, and the cycle repeats itself again and again. It's a downward spiral.

Chapter 4: Practical CBT Overview: Do It Yourself CBT

In this chapter, I'm just going to give you a quick overview of the succeeding chapters. Each chapter is going to drill down on each topic mentioned below.

This chapter is intended as an overview of what you're going to see in succeeding chapters. It also should help you map out how you are going to practice CBT on yourself.

Please note that this book teaches individuals from all walks of life how to practice cognitive behavioral therapy on themselves. This book is not intended for people looking to go through a formal CBT therapy session with a trained psychologist or licensed social worker.

While you are definitely free to do that, this book is aimed primarily at people who want to sort their issues out themselves using a CBT framework.

Please note that if you are already under the care of a licensed social worker, psychiatrist or psychologist, keep them in the loop. Tell them what you're doing because this may have an impact on whatever therapies you are already on.

Regardless, it's always a good idea to let your primary care provider know what kind of therapeutic systems you are exploring or have already implemented.

Here is a quick overview of the sections that we will discuss in detail in succeeding chapters:

- Take Inventory of Your Beliefs
- Understand the Power of Your Beliefs
- Be Honest About Your Belief's Impact
- Take Ownership of Your Beliefs
- Choose Alternatives That are Neutral or Positive
- Choose to Be Conscious

Just how much of an impact does a self-planned, independently implemented CBT program have on a person's overall outcome? Well, in a meta analysis conducted by Rober King, psychology professor at Queensland University of Technology in Australia, fifteen studies all point to the conclusion that there's really not much difference in ultimate outcomes for patients who worked with a therapist and those who just simply read a self-help book such as this or enrolled in an online program.

These patients were seeking treatment or were being treated for depression, obsessive-compulsive disorder, post-traumatic stress disorder and anxiety.

This is an interesting study to keep in mind, but please note that this is a meta analysis. Meaning, Professor King sampled existing studies and saw the patterns that they had in common.

Chapter 5: Take Inventory of Your Beliefs

Ask yourself, "what do I really believe about myself"?

Now, this is a big question because it can apply to so many different things. Let me walk you through the sub-questions you need to ask yourself.

What do you believe about yourself? This is the heart of whatever issue you are grappling with.

Did you know that all of us have a mental image of ourselves locked away in our minds? Some people have a clearer image than others, but we all have this image. It has an effect on how we choose to think, what we think about, how we respond, and our self esteem or self image.

These beliefs are not neutral. You have to ask yourself what you believe about yourself.

Now, to break this down, you can ask this subsidiary question: What do you really believe about who you are?

What are you capable of? What are you not capable of? What was your past like? What do you think your future would be like?

What is the point of your life? Is there a meaning to it? What is your life's purpose? Do you see yourself going somewhere in life? If so, where is it?

What have people given you in the past and what can you give to others? What are you capable of giving?

All these questions are interrelated because they all pick apart that image that you have in your mind. Now, it may not be a clear image, it may not always stand out and possibly even inform what you choose to think about and how you feel or how you behave, but it's there.

You have to keep asking yourself these questions because they ultimately lead to the question "Who do you think you are?"

It's interesting that most people don't even bother to stop and ask themselves this question. If they are struggling in any way or if they're feeling frustrated or they have certain challenges they can't seem to overcome, maybe it's due to the fact that they did not bother to stop and ask themselves these questions: Who am I? Who do I think I am?

These are two totally different questions. Who you are is an objective reality. Who do you think you are is a subjective question.

But believe it or not, your answer to the subjective questions impacts your objective reality. Because the moment you start changing your answer, you start changing your objective reality. Your emotional instincts change, yourself conception, self esteem, self image, all of those start to change. Ultimately, this leads to different emotional states and habits and leads to, of course, different actions.

Maybe that question is too big, so break it down. What do you really believe about yourself? What do you really believe about who you are? What are you capable of? What are you not capable of?

Are there any areas in your life that are off limits? If so, why are they off limits? Why are you holding yourself back from dreaming certain dreams or exploring certain ideas or planning certain things? Is there something about those goals that are just impossible or are these self imposed limitations?

You have to ask yourself these questions because no one can answer them except you. And until you answer these questions, it's going to be very hard for you to change because this question is crucial to cognitive behavioral therapy.

These questions list out the beliefs that you have. These beliefs may be holding you back. These beliefs may be setting up an artificial reality that prevents you from living up to your fullest potential.

You have to understand that, at some level or another, reality is only as real as your willingness to believe in it. Question your beliefs. But before you can get there, you have to first be aware of your beliefs. In other words, do an inventory.

This Requires Honesty

Now comes the hard part. It's very easy to delude ourselves. It's very easy to tell ourselves comforting stories about who we are, who we should be, the things that we should be doing and the things that we are doing. It's very easy to fool ourselves.

If you think about it, this is the reason why we are able to put up with a lot of unhappiness, discomfort and frustration in our lives. Because if we're fully honest with ourselves, we would stand up and say to ourselves, in clear terms, "I'm not happy. This is not working out. I know I deserve better. I know I'm capable of so much more. This is not acceptable."

But that's too harsh. That's too inconvenient. It begs the question of, "How hard am I willing to work to change things around?"

Faced with that question, most people shrink back. Most people want to run away from that question. I mean, you don't have to have an IQ of 120 or over to understand that question. People of average intelligence can see that a mile away.

So most people come up with excuses. We start looking at reality in a different way. We read our reality in such a way that we don't have to ask that question. And this is precisely what honesty destroys.

Because if you asked the earlier questions that we covered above and answered them honestly, a lot of your beliefs are going to come crashing down because it turns out that you simply put up these beliefs to get away from the harsh realities of your life.

The harsh reality is that you're not living up to your fullest potential. The harsh reality is that you may not be applying yourself the way you should be applying yourself. The harsh reality may be that you are settling for certain things.

Maybe you're doing it out of family obligation, maybe you're doing it because of low self esteem – there are just a million reasons why we settle. But it requires a lot of self deception to keep the system going.

When you choose to be honest, you start slashing away at all the comforting lies you tell yourself. This is the point when you start looking reality in the eye.

And the obvious reality is that you are not happy. You're not content. You are frustrated at some level or another, otherwise, you won't be reading this book. There would be no reason for you to read this book if everything was going well.

Honesty requires objective honesty. This means that you have to look at your life from the perspective of an outsider. Because if you don't do that, you will always be pulled in by the gravitational pull of the comforting lies, self deception, denial and excuses as well as justifications you have set up.

Because if it weren't for these, you would be forced to look at what's wrong in your life. You will be forced to take action.

Most people don't want to do that. They don't want to answer the question that is being begged to ask. They don't want to answer the question that's coming next.

Honesty means not only objective reality, but also getting away from answers that you think others expect you to give. It also requires answers that may be different from the answers that your parents have taught you. In other words, you have to go beyond tradition, obligation and custom. This is some heavy stuff, but it's absolutely necessary.

Write Down Your Beliefs

Again, go back to the central questions that I asked earlier. Write them down. Don't edit yourself. Just write down the first thing that comes to mind. It may be grammatically incorrect, it may be a run-on sentence, but it doesn't matter. Just get it down in writing.

Please understand that this is a process that is not going to take place at one time. It's not like you're carrying all these questions and you're just going to unload at one time. No. Expect this to play out over several days or even weeks.

Once you have everything down, clean up your list. Take out the duplicates, tighten up the sentences, and join similar statements. At the end of the process, you should have a clean, clear and concise list. There are no duplicates, they're easy to understand, and they are in plain English.

Again, don't expect this to happen overnight. Give yourself the space and the time to do this right.

Understand the Power of Your Beliefs

Now that you have your beliefs right in front of you in clear, black ink against a white background, pay attention to their power. You're not just looking at letters, you're not just staring into ink on paper. This is the script of your life, believe it or not. Your beliefs have an impact on what you do.

As I mentioned in my description of the emotional roller coaster that you're on, when you perceive certain stimuli from the outside world, it is your beliefs that help you form your thoughts.

Let's put it this way, if you did not believe in certain things or if you believed otherwise, then your thoughts would be different. This is not emotionally neutral because your thoughts trigger emotions, which trigger words, which can trigger actions. Once you take action, your world changes because the world only pays attention to your actions.

That's how you change your world. Accordingly, your beliefs have an impact on your ability to change your world. It directly impacts your reality, whether you accept it or not and whether you are conscious of it or not.

Now, you have a list of these beliefs that form your life's operating system. The computer or mobile device that you are using to read this book runs on OS. Your beliefs are your life's OS.

Please note that these beliefs are real in the sense that they're not just manifested in your feelings. You don't just feel good or bad when you think about these beliefs. They have an impact on what you do. They also impact what you feel you can or cannot do. Most importantly, they impact who you think you are and who you think you're not. Heavy stuff.

Pick through your beliefs with these impacts in mind. Understand that when you put everything together, you get a clear understanding of what your comfort zone is. You get to see the outlines of your personal limits. This is that imaginary line that you set for yourself.

You say to yourself that within this line, everything is possible. Outside of this line, things are going to be very difficult, there are going to be a lot of challenges, and sometimes, things are just not possible.

Understand where that line is. You will only be able to get that when you read through your beliefs over and over again. Then and only then would you be able to connect the dots, and the broad outlines of your comfort zone start to appear.

Please note that at this stage, we're talking theory. In Chapter 6, we're going to discuss the types of impact these beliefs have on you and what you can do about them.

In a 2008 study out of the Brazilian university Universidade Federal do Rio Grande do Sul (UFRGS) led by researcher Paulo Knapp, CBT treatments and therapy were determined to have been more effective when participants wrote down their beliefs honestly and clearly. These findings were published in the journal SCiElo.

Similarly, in a 2017 study out of the University of Pennsylvania published by Cheryl Joy Easterbrook, researchers studied the importance of honesty and authenticity during CBT therapy sessions. They saw a tight link between the level of honesty and authenticity of the subjects and the effectiveness of their treatment.

Finally, in a research that was published by Duke University in 2015, researcher Dr. Harold Koenig indicated that religious belief played a very big role in determining the effectiveness of depression therapy. Koenig saw a positive correlation between religiosity or level or religious belief and responsiveness to depression therapy. His findings were published in The Journal of Nervous and Mental Disease. This was a 2015 study.

Chapter 6: Be Honest about Your Beliefs' Impact

At this point, you probably already know firsthand that it's very hard to accept certain beliefs you have about your life. Put more precisely, it's very hard to accept that you believe certain things about your life.

Maybe it's embarrassing. Perhaps it doesn't quite line up to what other people expect you to believe. However, please understand that there is no right or wrong answer. What's important is that you are honest. There's really no right or wrong answer in terms of the content of your belief. What's important is that you are clear that you believe these things.

If you think that's hard because you realize that in many cases and at different levels, you believe in all sorts of idealized images of who you are or what you're about, etc.

It gets even worse. Why? In this chapter, you're going to have to be honest about the impact of those beliefs. It's hard enough accepting that you believe certain things about yourself. It's going to be harder to reconcile with the consequences of those beliefs.

Please understand that this is absolutely necessary so you can get a big picture view of what you're doing to your life. There, I said it. I did not say what your parents did to you. I did not say what your ex-partner did to you. I'm talking about what you're doing to your life.

This has nothing to do with past bosses, past situations you were in, your upbringing, none of that. Instead, everything that we're going to talk about involves the impact of your choice. I know this is really hard to accept. Who in their right minds would choose to be miserable? What sane person would choose to be powerless, voiceless and, let's face it, ineffective in life?

However, that's precisely what's going on if we're completely honest here. Remember there are certain parts of your life that you have designated "no-go zones". In fact, if you look at the big picture, it may well turn out that most of the things that are possible in your life are not available to you.

This doesn't mean that they're physically impossible but you have made them off-limits. Okay? Let's get that out of the way.

In this chapter we're going to talk about the impact of your beliefs. These cannot be denied. These cannot be swept under the rug. The sooner you get a clear understanding of what these are and how they hold you back and drag you down from living up to your fullest potential, the better.

What are You Afraid of?

Did you know that your beliefs impact your fears? If you believe certain things are possible and other things are impossible, this is going to have an effect on what you choose to be afraid of.

Please understand that most adults are not afraid of scary monsters under their bed. Instead, they're afraid of trying. They're afraid of making an effort or planning something up that falls outside of their comfort zone.

In many cases, they're afraid of dreaming big dreams that take them outside of their comfort zone. I want you to focus on the things that you're afraid of. What are the things that you say that you're just not capable of or that's just not going to happen?

Are you afraid of becoming rich or are you afraid of putting in the work that is necessary to become rich? These are two totally different things.

Are you afraid of being famous or are you afraid of saying and doing things that may be unpopular that will help you become more noteworthy? Which is it?

Look at all the different areas of your life, and I'm talking about your professional life, your business life, your education, your relationships, your health, everything, and ask yourself, "What am I afraid of in these areas of my life? What conclusions, what realities am I trying to run away from?

What are You Waiting for?

Did you know that when you believe certain things about yourself you end up postponing personal victory? Let's put it this way. If you think that you are not smart enough or you don't have the skills that you need for ultimate success, you trick yourself into thinking that you have to wait for certain things to fall into place before you can learn what you need to learn or before things are possible for you.

I know it sounds crazy. It sounds illogical but this is exactly what a lot of people do. What they're really doing is they're giving themselves excuse after excuse not to do anything right here right now. They're kicking the can down the road.

That's what they're doing, and one of the most common manifestations of this is the idea that they're waiting for somebody else to make a move, for the opportunity to present itself, for them to feel just right or for things to fall into place. Excuse after excuse after excuse.

Please understand that the more you wait, the closer you are to death. I know that's an unpleasant topic, but every single day that you wake up, you get one day closer to your death. You're not going to live forever.

Your life's clock does not have unlimited time. Sooner or later, you're going to run out of time. This is precisely why you need to stop waiting. To get there, you have to ask yourself, "What am I waiting for?"

This is an extremely important consequence of your beliefs. The fact that you are living your life in anticipation of something that doesn't come means you believe in certain things.

What's Holding You Back?

Did you know that the human mind is the most powerful biochemical machine in existence? We can edit our reality just by selecting our thoughts. A lot of people do not want to claim that power. Why? With great power comes responsibility.

Great power means exercise. You're going to have to exercise that power. That's why they'd rather hold back. They'd rather say, "Well, it's just not the right time or I don't know enough or, worse yet, I don't have that power to begin with". You can be whoever you want to be. You can achieve whatever you want to achieve.

I know it's not popular to say this because we would all rather like to hear the fiction that there are certain things in life that are just off-limits to us. There's something comforting about the idea that human beings are essentially powerless at some level or other. However, if I said those things to you, I would be lying to you because the truth is the opposite.

Whatever other people can do, you can do too. You just need to focus. We would like to dismiss all the success that other people are enjoying by saying that they have certain advantages. We would like to believe in the fiction that they just happen to be at the right place at the right time to know the right things with the right people to get the right results.

However, you have to understand that you can achieve those things as well. It doesn't matter what color your skin is. It doesn't matter how old you are. It doesn't matter whether you're a male or a female, whether you're trans or cis gender. It doesn't matter whether you are regularly able or physically challenged. None of that matters.

These are excuses. These are artificial barriers that we hide behind to hold us back from doing the things we know we're capable of doing. This is a moment of honesty so ask yourself what is holding you back. Put more precisely, what do you choose to believe in that holds you back? What is your crutch?

Is it the fact that your parents did not have much money when they were raising you? Is it the fact that you came from a developing country? Is it the fact that your English skills are not as polished as they could be?

What is it? List these down. Be fully aware of these. After you've listed them down, see them for the lies that they are. They are excuses or flat-out lies. You know it, I know it, everybody knows it.

What's holding you back?

Who Do You Think will "Save" You?

This is not a theological question. I'm just asking this question solely in human terms. A lot of people might be thinking, "This is crazy. Why would people think that somebody out there is going to save them?"

Well, if you're really honest, this is how people think. Somehow some way they think at some level or other there is some sort of lifeline that their buddy or their friend or somebody they know will show up at the right time at the right place to produce the right outcome or they think that the answer lies in the hands of somebody else. Once that person shows up, they save the day.

These are excuses you give yourself because there's no person out there who will save you except yourself. Again, I'm talking about practical terms here. I'm not talking theologically.

You have to take the first move. You have to take the initiative. You can't sit around and expect somebody to save you. That's just not going to happen. Yes, this even applies to people who say they love you. This extends to people who say that you complete them.

Why? Everybody's got enough problems of their own. At the end of the day, everybody has to take care of number one. Isn't it time you took care of number one? Stop looking for a savior. Instead, step up and understand that this is your responsibility to yourself.

Your Beliefs are the Foundations of All the Questions Above

If you answer these questions honestly, you would realize that what you choose to believe has real consequences for your conceptions of who you are, what you're capable of, your personal limits, the ideal relationship, your values and your character.

It all begins with what you choose to believe. If you think that you are a victim, that's going to have an impact in how you deal with other people. What if I told you that victims tend to be the biggest victimizers?

It's easy to figure this out. Think about it. If you think that other people have victimized you in the past, this is all the excuse you need to victimize others. It's easy to say, "Well, I was abused so it's okay to abuse others. I was stolen from so it's okay to steal from others. I'm the victim here."

Be aware of your beliefs and their impact on your other beliefs. Ultimately, this translates to the life that you are living. It translates to the things that you think you can or cannot do. It translates to whether you think life is one grand open adventure full of possibility or just a prison with invisible walls.

Ultimately, it's your choice. How do you make that choice? You choose your beliefs. Your beliefs are real.

How Your Beliefs Impact Your Physical Life

You may be thinking that this is all philosophical, that these are just conjecture and theory. Well, here's how it plays out. As I mentioned earlier, every single second you're picking up thousands of stimuli from the outside world. These are the things that you see, hear, touch, taste and smile. Interestingly enough, you only choose to be aware of a tiny fraction of all the stimuli the world throws your way. Of these things that you are aware of, you only think about a tiny sunset. You interpret these based on your beliefs.

Again, back to the case of the expensive car. If you believe that you are small, powerless and need some sort of patron or savior, it's easy for you to say, "I can't afford that". When that happens, you're basically saying, "I am free from having to change what I'm doing to get what I want".

You're also saying to yourself, "I can't dream big. That's for other people, not for me. I'm a victim. I need to be saved by somebody else. Somebody has stuff and it is through the kindness of their heart that they will share it with me, but the only way I can get that stuff is through other people". You feel small, weak, voiceless and at the mercy of other people.

Is this the mindset of a powerful person? Is this the mindset of a person who looks at the world as something that he or she can bend to his or her will? Of course not. This is the mindset of a defeated person. This is how people who live in personal prisons with invisible walls think. I know this is not easy to hear but it needs to be said.

Understand that your beliefs are real. They impact how you think about your stimuli which is your analysis, and this translates to an emotional state which impacts what you talk about, how you talk about things and, most importantly, your actions.

The solution is simple. It is as simple as it is clear. If you want to change your actions for the better and if you want to live life as a victor, you have to stop thinking like a victim. In other words, you have to change the analysis you use when you perceive certain things.

Please understand that a lot of this is internal. A lot of this involves your feelings and most of it involves your thoughts.

However, the world only cares about your actions. The world could not care less about what you're feeling. Everybody's got feelings. Join the club. The world couldn't care less about your intentions and motivations.

You know what it sits up and pays attention to? It pays attention to your actions. This is why it's really important to understand your beliefs and their impact on you and choose your beliefs wisely.

Choose how you think because ultimately how you think needs to leads to how you act and, at that point, the world punishes or rewards you depending on your actions. Wouldn't it be great?

Change is Possible through CBT

Wouldn't it be great to change your beliefs so they don't lead to stress, anxiety, depression, phobias, procrastination, constantly comparing yourself to others and low self-esteem?

Believe it or not, you can change your belief system. You can reprogram your mind so that once you get triggered by certain stimuli, you don't automatically have to feel bad, assume the worst and take negative action. You don't have to continue to live with negative feedback loops. In other words, you can break out of a negative chain reaction or emotional downward spirals.

In a 2003 study at the University of Sydney in Australia, researcher James Bennett-Levy discovered that when patients clearly identified their irrational beliefs, they were able to change them during cognitive behavioral therapy treatments. This led to an improvement in patients with depression.

In another study out of Newcastle University in the United Kingdom, Stephen Barton showed that core personal fundamental beliefs can actually be changed using cognitive behavioral therapy techniques.

Finally, out of VU University Amsterdam in the Netherlands, Ellen Driessen published in 2011 a study that clearly showed how mood disorders can be effectively treated through belief modification. In the study, patients and therapists identified the patients' beliefs regarding a problem and patients showed improvement when they were able to cope effectively with their beliefs.

Chapter 7: Take Ownership of Your Beliefs

At this point, it's very easy to feel discouraged. First of all, you realize that you believe certain things that may be embarrassing. It may well turn out that you believe in certain things that are very self-destructive as far your mood, emotions self-esteem go.

You also may feel a heavy burden brought on by the realization that these beliefs have a tremendous impact in your identity, your self-esteem and your self-confidence. This all may seem too heavy. It might even feel like you've picked all these apart and became aware of them too soon.

Well, here's the hardest part. You're going to have to take ownership of your beliefs. That's the bottom line. This chapter is going to be very short because it really all boils down to one action: taking ownership.

If you're able to make it past this point, CBT becomes really easy. Seriously. It becomes a cakewalk. This is the hardest part. You have to take ownership of your beliefs. I'm not talking about just intellectual ownership like you're sitting back in a college classroom and the professor or instructor introduces a new concept and you got it. I'm not talking about intellectual acceptance or intellectual understanding.

Taking ownership of your beliefs must not just make sense in your mind but make sense in your heart as well. You have to believe this truly. You have to develop a sense of urgency. You can't just safely compartmentalize this in your mind as some sort of intellectual agenda item. In other words, it requires commitment.

You know it's funny. People talk about all sorts of key concepts and get all excited about it. It's easy to get excited when we're just kicking around ideas.

For example, when planning a business during a brainstorming session and everybody is trying to be a hero. Everybody comes up with all sorts of ideas. They're all excited about how clever they are.

However, once it comes down to making a commitment and taking ownership of certain ideas and running with them all the way through, people get cold feet. People start walking back their hot ideas. People start getting wishy-washy.

This is the moment of truth. You have a clear understanding of what your beliefs are. You understand how they impact you negatively. Now is the time to do something about it. You have to take ownership, and this is not just intellectual ownership where you knowledge that you believe in certain things that are bad for you or have negative effects. It requires more than that. It requires committing to the following.

First, you will have to say and believe "I will not make excuses". This is going to be hard. It really is. Why? Think about it. When you have an excuse, you don't have to take action. It's that simple.

When you say "I will not make excuses", you have taken that off the table. Now, you have to take action. Now you have to take responsibility. Worse yet, now how you have to follow through. You have to commit to this. No excuses whatsoever.

At the end of the day, the buck stops with you because it's your life. You can't spend the rest of your life pointing a finger at your parents, at bad things that happened in the past, at the schoolyard bully, at that mean boss who did not understand you. They don't matter. You have to live with your left, and that's why it's really important to say and believe "I will not make excuses anymore".

Next, there are many perfectly understandable justifications for why your life has taken the direction it did. There are certain things beyond your control. These are objectively true but you know what? Forget them. Turn your back on them. Instead, say to yourself, "I will not take shelter in justifications. Again, the buck stops with you.

Next, say to yourself, "I will not engage in historicism". The funny thing about relationships is that oftentimes when we get into a heated argument with our loved ones, we not only get hysterical but we also get historical. We dig up all sorts of bad decisions that they made, all the bad things that they said and did just to score points.

At this point, you're going to turn your back on all of that. You're going to say to yourself I will not engage in historicism. The past is dead. I'm going to focus on right here, right now so I can have a better future.

Stop using the past as a crutch. Stop using it as some sort of toolbox to make you feel good today or to give you an excuse in avoiding hard choices today. The past is the past. It offers very important lessons but let it be the past.

Finally, you have to say to yourself, "I promise to myself I will play no games". This is the last part in taking ownership over your beliefs. You know what your beliefs are. You know how toxic they are to you. You know their negative effects.

It is time to stop playing games. It is time to stop waiting for people to change. It's hard enough trying to change yourself. Can you imagine trying to change other people? Do you really think that when you feel bad, hurt or angry at them that they will change? No, they won't. They have other things to do. They have enough problems of their own.

The world continues to turn on its axis. You have to do the same. Stop playing games. Understand that you own everything in your life. It's all on you.

I know you're not supposed to say that. We're not supposed to be self-centered. We're not supposed to think that we can do everything but, ultimately, when it comes to our beliefs and the massive impact our beliefs have on how our lives turn out, you have to do that. Take ownership. This means saying, "I am responsible. I have the power to respond in the way I choose. I can always choose".

Again, this is not just stuff to make you feel good. This is not just intellectual realizations. This is not algebra or calculus. This is real life so this means that you have to commit. This has to translate into actual action and decisions.

Here's the step-by-step approach that you need to take so you can fully take ownership of your beliefs.

Step #1: Take Ownership

When you do this, you basically say yourself, "I own my beliefs". This doesn't mean somebody planted these beliefs in me or I just copied my parents, I just followed out of obligation or I just did this as a coping mechanism. No. Stop saying those things.

Just say, "I own my beliefs. One hundred percent. Lock, stock and barrel. Now that I have taken ownership, I can change them". Do you see how this works?

If you do not own your beliefs, then you are just waiting for the actual owners to get their act together. Do you realize how impossible that is? They've moved on.

The schoolyard body who humiliated you in front of everybody? He's moved on. Your ex who cheated on you and crushed your self-esteem? He or she has moved on. Your boss who humiliated you by making you feel dumb? He has moved on.

Take ownership of your beliefs. Beliefs came from those negative experiences. Those traumatic chapters in your past shape your beliefs. Take ownership of those beliefs right here, right now because if you don't, you will never be able to change them. You will always be at the mercy of the past or people in situations you cannot control. You will always remain frustrated, powerless, small.

The bottom line is if you spend a ridiculous portion of your time blaming other people for what went wrong in your life, you're simply handing them power over your life.

Logically, whatever caused the problem can fix the problem. Since you're so busy blaming other people, then you're essentially training yourself to say "Wait for the solution from them". That's not going to happen. Stop it. Take ownership.

I know you're not at fault. I know you're feeling like a victim. I know you have the wounds and the scars to show for it, but it doesn't matter. Take ownership right here, right now so you can change them.

Step #2: Test Your Beliefs

What are the facts that your assumptions and beliefs are based on? If you think you're ugly or unattractive or dumb, what are the facts that these beliefs are based on? If you think you you're a bad partition or you're a victim, can you point the certain things that happened in your past that gave rise to these conclusions because that's all they are. They are conclusions.

Please understand that facts are not feelings I want you to look for facts. I don't want you to say, "Well, I've felt really bad! I felt really small and I was scared!" No, that's not going to take you anywhere. What are the facts that led to your belief?

Here's the key question, "Did they really happen?" Believe it or not there is such a thing as a false memory. If you dig deep enough, a lot of the memories that you think form the foundation of certain core beliefs you have about yourself, your capabilities, your value as a person, your ability to love, so on and so forth may not have happened at all. Maybe they were a dream. Perhaps somebody said them to you.

However, they're not things that actually took place. They were not things that you could have seen, heard, smelled, tasted or touched. You'd be surprised as to how much of your beliefs are rooted in things that simply did not happen.

Next, did they happen to the degree you "remember" them? Even if your belief is based on something that actually took place, did things really take place the way you remember them or are you blowing things up out of proportion?

I remember reminiscing with my brother about that one time we got into a fight with a bunch of guys, and my brother kept emphasizing the fact that a guy that we still both knew hit me in the back of the head. I remember for a fact that when that happened, I didn't make a big deal out of it.

However, several years back when my brother kept saying that this was a friend of ours, that we knew him and it was basically a form betrayal, it started to eat into me. Then slowly but surely when I thought back to that event, my interpretation of that experience became worse and worse from a simple fight that people have when they were kids to an early experience of betrayal, backstabbing, manipulation, deception and other very negative "truths".

It turned out that I absorbed my brother's interpretation and made it my personal truth. Look at all the facts that form the bedrock of your personal assumptions and ask yourself, "Am I exaggerating certain things? Am I pointing the "camera" of my memory a certain way to emphasize certain things or de-emphasize other details?

Finally, are you reading in the very worst into your memory? Even if things actually happened, are you filling in certain details that make the memory more poisonous than it needs to be?

Go through all of these questions when confronting the facts underlying your assumptions. You'd be surprised as to how many of your assumptions and beliefs are based on facts that did not happen, are exaggerated or are simply "filled in".

Step #3: Perform the "So What?" Test

If things did happen in the worst way possible, ask yourself, "So what?" Ask yourself that question. At first, it's going to be a shock. It's going to be very hard to move on at this point, but you have to do it. Oftentimes, when people ask themselves "So what?", it's as if somebody slapped them across the face and scales fell out of their eyes. They start to see perspective.

When you say the words "So what?", you shift the camera of your memory from you being the center of the universe to the rest of the universe. You start seeing context. You regain perspective.

I understand "So what?" is a sharp question. You may feel devalued, even insulted, but you have to ask yourself that question, "So what?"

When you do this, you give yourself a moment of decision. You have to decide to move on despite what happened. Again, you only ask yourself this question if things actually turn out the way you thought they turn out.

It's based on facts. There's not reinterpretation. There's no exaggeration. There's nothing to fill in. This actually happened and then your beliefs arose from those facts. Once you find yourself in this position, drop the bomb. Ask "So what?"

This gives you a point of decision. You give yourself the chance to move on despite what happened. What exactly do you do? Well, you stop reading the worst interpretation into your life. You also stop blowing things out of proportion.

Once you do that, you focus on what really happened and understand that it is negative, but you decide as an exercise of personal will and focus to just let it go.

Yes, that very pretty girl in your sixth grade class, Tina, said you're ugly. So what?

Yes, your favorite professor thought you were dumb and dismissed all your ideas. So what?

Yes, your best friend screwed around on you. So what?

This is painful. It's definitely not something people would volunteer for but, at the end of the day, you have to decide to let it go. Let go because these facts form beliefs that make your life toxic. Let go of these facts, build new beliefs and enjoy the new life these new beliefs make possible.

In a 2017 study from Universitas Muria Kudus led by Ridwa Pramono, CBT techniques that involved acknowledging and testing one's personal beliefs led to self-understanding, which helped adolescent orphans in an orphanage, accept themselves better. These findings were published in the Bentham journal.

Similarly, a study out of the Department of Psychiatry at the University Medical Center Hamburg-Eppendorf, lead researcher Christian Otte published in 2011 a study that showed that when people let go of fear and negative beliefs, their anxiety disorder symptoms were reduced.

Finally, out of the University of Rochester in 2010, a research group led by Mary Tantillo showed that when people suffering from eating disorders tested their beliefs, it helps them overcome the underlying issues that produce their eating disorders. This study was published in ScienceDirect.

Chapter 8: Choose Alternatives That Are Neutral Or Positive

In the previous chapter, we talked about testing your beliefs by using factual analysis. It takes a lot of willpower. Please understand that the technique described in Chapter 7 doesn't come easy. How can it? You're reprogramming how your mind works. You're going to be going up against the mental habits you have developed up to that point in time. A leopard after all doesn't change its spots at least not overnight.

It can happen. You just have to stick to it. Eventually you should be able to handle stimuli in such a way that you will always be in control of your mood. Again, this doesn't come easy. It is not second nature. Still, if you mastered the technique that I'm going to teach you below, cognitive behavioral therapy will help you become a more positive, upbeat, and yes, more effective person.

Whatever is frustrating you or dragging you down is simply a function of how you interpret stimuli. We've already established this many times before in this book. Please understand that it all goes back to the same central fact: you are always analyzing the stimuli in your life. This is a key part of living. You're always making judgment calls. You're always thinking about the things that you choose to be aware of. This is always going to happen.

The big opportunity here is that it doesn't have to happen the same way as it did before. You're reading this book because the way you interpret your stimuli leads you to a bad place. Maybe you feel small, stuck, powerless, voiceless, or angry. Maybe you feel depressed, discouraged, and constantly disappointed. It doesn't have to be this way. By learning how to analyze otherwise neutral stimuli in your life a certain way, you take more control over your life. Here's how it works.

Choose Empowering Explanations

Whenever you perceive stimuli, you are explaining natural phenomena. You're trying to fit them into your explanation of how the world works. This is never neutral nor is it inherited. Don't think that just because you're doing it a certain way that everybody else is doing it the same exact way as you. We are all products of our backgrounds, our experiences, and yes, our attitudes. Understand that you are currently explaining your world to yourself a certain way.

Obviously, it doesn't lead to results you're happy with either. Otherwise, you won't be reading this book. You would not be reading this book. Maybe the explanations or analysis that you've come up with are self-defeating or negative. Actively choose empowering explanations. This is extremely important. You're always explaining the world to yourself. Be aware of this fact. Be clear about the explanations that you give to yourself.

Do they empower you? Do they take you to the next level? Do they give you a sense of ownership over your life? Or do they make you feel small, voiceless, powerless, stuck, weak, flawed, ugly, fat, dumb, and repugnant? These are all choices. I know it doesn't feel like a choice because it seems like the moment you detect something, it's as if you got on a roller coaster and there's really not much you can do from that point on.

Believe me, I understand that. But if you want to create changes in your life, you have to freeze the process. You already perceived the stimuli. That's not the problem. Stimuli inherently are neutral. The big issue here is how do you explain that to yourself. How mindful are you of the explanations you're giving yourself? Do these explanations lead you to somewhere you want to go?

Choose Empowering Assumptions

Assumptions and explanations are joined at the hip. Usually, once you start explaining things to yourself or you're really trying to fit in the stimuli that you have perceived or have become aware of to what you know previously, you're making certain assumptions. The moment you make an explanation, you can bet that you are triggering your assumptions. Somehow someway, you are using your assumptions.

Explanations after all don't come out of nowhere. You have to choose your assumptions carefully. Ask yourself if your assumptions make you feel empowered and able. Alternatively, do they make you feel powerless, weak, or voiceless? Does it seem like your life is just a movie that you cannot change. The best thing you can do is just to plop down into your seat, lean back, and watch the movie of your life play out in front of you. This is some assumption. Obviously, other people can have different assumptions. Change your assumptions and you change your explanations. Change your explanations and you change your results. That's how it works.

Take the case of John. John went to a bar to get some drinks with friends. As John entered, a very attractive female near the middle of the room started laughing at John's direction. She was looking straight at John. At this point, John can assume that she is laughing at him. His explanation for this then is that he is somehow some way ugly, repugnant, or otherwise, unattractive.

It doesn't take a rocket scientist to figure out that this doesn't exactly to a healthy self-esteem. How do you think John would respond in that situation if those were his assumptions and explanations to himself?

He would probably quickly shrink like a violet and make a beeline to the back of the room or hightail it back to his apartment. He would feel small, rejected, ugly, unattractive, unwanted, isolated, alone and broken.

With this set of assumptions and explanations, it's very easy for John to be depressed. And worse yet his self-confidence will take a hit. So when the next time he goes to that same bar or any other type of social setting where there are attractive members of the opposite sex, he'd be gone shy when it comes to approaching females.

That memory probably would stick to him. Over time, he probably would exaggerate that memory and gets worse and worse. But what if we go back to that point in time when John entered the bar. Imagine there's CCTV footage of us. As we go through the footage, we freeze that point in time when the female starts laughing. We take a look at her eyes. We take a look at the angle of her face.

Low and behold, it may well turn out that she was not laughing at John directly but the guy behind John. Maybe the guy was wearing a funny hat or cracking a joke or acting in a goofy way to get attention. With this crucial piece of information may well turn out that she wasn't laughing at John. This had nothing to do with John. You are John. All of us are John.

We have a choice. We can read what happened in the worst way possible or we can interpret them to at least neutralize negativity. The most neutral reading of this is that she was laughing at somebody else. The most positive reading of this is she was looking and laughing at what somebody behind John did but was still looking at John.

So there was some sort of attraction there. Regardless, you are responsible for how you read the facts of your life. Are you going to interpret them in such a way that you remain feeling small, unwanted, lonely, frustrated and disappointed? Or are you going to read them in a way that makes you empowered? Focus on your choice. If anything that is what you should focus on because when you shine a spotlight on your choice and your ability to choose, you focus on your personal power to turn things around, to live the life that you want for yourself, and ultimately master your own personal reality.

This illustration using the character of John is born out by research. In a 2014 study out of the University of Torso, Norway led by Jens C. Thimm, the research team found that when people look at a situation from a positive perspective, they are able to overcome depression. Thimm's team examined this phenomenon in the context of CBT. Their findings were published in the Journal Biomedical Central Psychiatry.

Similarly, in a study out of Bergen, Norway published in 2013 by Silje Reme discovered that when workers who are struggling with work participation changed their attitude towards work and switched their thoughts about work from negative to positive, they achieved better results. Finally, in the PLOS Journal, a research study conducted by Anna Hugued from Dalhousie University, apps programmed with exercises that coached patients to think positively enabled these individuals to overcome depression. Make no mistake. Your assumptions regarding a situation leads to certain explanations that can either push you up or drag you down.

Chapter 9: Choose To Be Conscious

One of the greatest features of CBT is that it is a fully conscious exercise. You're not put under hypnosis. Your ability to detect reality does not suffer. You don't enter an altered state of mind. Instead, you are fully conscious about the whole process. This maximizes your sense of control and ownership over the way you look at life- the way you look at and exercise life. CBT enables people to become more conscious of their life. Here are some exercises you can use to maximize your consciousness.

The more conscious you are, the clearer your thinking patterns become. You need a high level of clarity to realize that you are interpreting and explaining the things happening in your life the wrong way. Using this clarity, you can then introduce different assumptions and explanations that can change your mood and by extension change your emotional state and your actions. Consider the following exercises.

Select Affirmations That Sum Up Your Greater Focus In Autonomy

Come up with the affirmations that put your power to choose your personal reality front and center. Now, this may seem hokey. The stereotype is somebody sitting in front of a mirror and saying I am a good person. People like me. That kind of stuff. Well, you don't have to treat this like some sort of a mantra. There is really no one right answer.

Focus instead on affirmations that make sense to you. Everybody is different. Everybody has a different set of personal circumstances. Focus on affirmations that enhance your focus and boosts your sense of autonomy. Focus on concepts involving choice and the ability to set your own standards to go your own way. Again, everybody's different. So I'm not going to feed you with canned affirmation. You have to figure this out yourself.

Make It A Habit To Say These Affirmations At Least Once A Day

When you do it, don't go through the motions. Be intentional when you don't. Listen to every word that you verbalize. Imagine the words coming to life. Apply them in certain hypotheticals in your mind. The worst way you can do this is to treat it like a mantra. Basically, you just go through the motions. You rattle off these 'magic words' and expect some sort of miracle.

It doesn't work that way. Instead, this is a lived experience that results in your active and conscious reprogramming of how your mind works. Heavy stuff, right? Well, treat it accordingly. The reason why a lot of people like to dismiss affirmations is because of the fact that it actually requires work and focus. Done properly, it can change your life. It doesn't take effect overnight. It is something that you perfect over time. Don't hesitate to tweak your affirmations and customize them.

Think Like A Director

Another way you can increase your ability to consciously focus on things happening in your life and your mind's ability to explain phenomena happening in your life is to think like a director. When you perceive certain things or you get triggered by a memory from the past, freeze each frame.

Ask yourself what am I thinking at this point.

What is my explanation and what are the assumptions behind those explanations? When you do this, you clinically dissect how you think. You don't give yourself a pass. You don't assume anything. You look at what you perceived and how you interpreted that perception. This is a very powerful way of editing your mental processes.

It takes a lot of work and attention to detail. But when you get good at it, your sense of control over your mind and your moment by moment consciousness explodes. It really does. It's difficult but the payoff is just amazing because the sense of mastery that you get enables you to essentially take control of your thoughts.

At least you can question them and this is often enough to throw you off your regular track. If your regular track leads to negativity, low self-esteem, and lower competence, you need to throw yourself off track. Thinking like a director and applying some sort of freeze frame perception to how you think goes a long way in helping you attain a great degree of mental and emotional control.

Think Like A Programmer

Another way you can boost your consciousness is to sit down with a piece of paper and then diagram your thought processes starting with the stimuli. This takes a tremendous amount of personal focus and discipline but it can be done. You start with a symbol for the stimuli and you draw an arrow to the next symbol which indicates your interpretation or your analysis of them.

You can break that down and and the arrow points to your emotional state which eventually leads to things you say and things you do. Again, this level of clarity doesn't happen overnight. But the more you diagram what's going on in your mind and how it affects your decisions, the greater the likelihood you will attain a sense of control. This is especially true if you notice that the diagram always ends up a certain way. You can do experiments to throw yourself off to see if you can end up with a better state of mind.

Always Remember This

Regardless of whether you select affirmations or you think like a director or a programmer, always remember that you are in control. I know it doesn't feel like it most of the time but this is the truth. You can always control the interpretation you choose for your thoughts. You can always choose to focus on certain facts and not others. This is tremendous. This is never trivial. Because everything you do.

Everything you feel. Everything you think about yourself as a human being flows from this skill. So, take this seriously. You are the gatekeeper to your mind. If you're having a tough time with all of these techniques, please understand that you have a lot to gain. If anything, you will end up in a better place than where you are now. You don't have to feel stuck, frustrated, let down, small, weak, powerless, ugly, and alone.

You don't have to constantly feel that you don't belong anywhere. Whatever personal challenge you are facing, understand that when you go through the process of applying all the techniques mentioned in this book, you will gain a much better life. Focus on what you stand to gain. I cannot emphasize this enough. It's easy to think that you're basically just pushing up against a mountain. It might seem impossible because after all you have grown accustomed to thinking a certain way.

It's never easy. Breaking habits is never easy. But you need to do it. And one way to get motivated and stay motivated is to focus on what you stand to gain with CBT. First, you get to free yourself from stress. When you use these exercises, free yourself from a tremendous amount of stress and pressure.

You free yourself from depression or a negative point of view that constantly drags you down. Depression is real. Even if it's not full-blown depression, it's still a real problem. Why? It reduces your energy level. It puts you in a position where you're more likely to interpret life very negatively. Focus on the sense of control that you get when you practice these exercises. That sense of control isn't just a nice happy feeling. It gives you hope. That's right. Hope. Remember that. With hope, you can look forward to a better tomorrow. Sure things may be chaotic right now and at some level or other, it burns you up. But there is light at the end of the tunnel. Things don't have to remain the same.

Chapter 10: Best Practices For More Optimal CBT Results

If you just follow the previous nine chapters, letter for letter and fully implemented those steps, you would be in a better position than you are now. Still, if you want to get the most out of the mental and emotional management skills you learned from CBT, you might want to do the following.

Keep A CBT Journal

Simply writing down what you're doing and your results can go a long way in helping you master CBT. At first your journal is probably going to be just a series of chaotic notes. Sooner or later, you will learn how to take note of the stuff that truly matters. You'll learn how to track your progress and at the very least, you get a nice little boost when you read your CBT diary.

How come? You can look at the past and see how much you were struggling then and compare it to how much better you are now that you are using CBT. If anything it gives you that nice little push to keep going. Remember CBT is a commitment. It's not a one time big time kind of approach. It's definitely not a one shot deal.

Practice Mindfulness

Mindfulness is very popular in the western world nowadays. A lot of people even confuse it with meditation. But mindfulness really is a bigger set of practices that contain meditation. Put it another way. Meditation is just a subset of mindfulness techniques. It's very important that you understand this because a lot of people are automatically turned off by mindfulness because they assume that it's exactly like Buddhist or Hindu meditation.

A lot of people nowadays are turned off by any kind of mysticism, spirituality, or anything that smacks of religion. But please understand that meditation is only a small subset of the greater set of practices called mindfulness. Here's a short list of mindfulness techniques that you may want to adopt. Quickly and briefly describe each mindfulness technique so you can investigate further.

Simple Breath Control

Did you know that by simply breathing in slowly and then holding your breath for maybe four to five seconds and then breathing back out and holding your breath, you can let go of a tremendous amount of stress? This is not conjecture. People who use simple breath control are able to not only de-stress almost immediately but they're also able to increase their focus.

Simple breath control for stress purposes was actually pioneered for use by U.S. Navy Seals troops. It's easy to see why. Seals carry out some of the most dangerous and precise military operations among all the U.S. Armed Forces. They need to stay focused. And they stay focused immediately by simply breathing slowly in and holding your breath for four to five or even six seconds and then breathing slowly out and then holding. After that, you quickly relax. Simply repeat this series for three to four times and you're good to go.

Counting Your Breath

When you close your eyes and focus all your attention on the breath leaving and entering your nostrils, you turn off all your other senses. You remain completely conscious but you're consciousness and ability to become aware are fine-tuned like a laser. You have to slowly breathe in and out. You have to repeat this for a few times until a sense of calm, peace, and serenity overcomes you.

Transcendental Meditation

With this mindfulness technique, you slowly breathe in and out with your eyes closed and then after a few repetitions, you breathe in and mentally recite a mantra. Now, at this point a lot of people start getting nervous because mantras after all are rooted in Hinduism or Buddhism but for transcendental meditation purposes, the mantra is different. The mantra actually is some sort of nonsense word that you yourself made up. It has to be nonsense.

Why? The whole point of transcendental meditation is to time your breathing to a word that does not trigger thought. When you keep using your mantra in line with breathing in and breathing out, thought is destroyed. That is the whole point of transcendental meditation. It allows you to transcend or rise above the level of thought. If you have a tough time separating your emotions from your thoughts, transcendental meditation can do wonders for you.

If you are a very unstable person emotionally, transcendental meditation can give you that piece that you're looking for. The key here is to find a mantra that you make up for yourself that doesn't trigger any thought. Eventually, a sense of calm, serenity, and harmony flows through as you repeat your mantra over and over.

Single Object Focus

If you don't have much time to meditate or practice mindfulness, single object focus is a quick way to achieve mindfulness. The whole point of a single object focus is to simply become aware of the present moment. You're not worrying about what will possibly happen in the future nor are you beating yourself up about what happened in the past.
Instead, you focus on the present. Single object focus enables you to think of the

present as an infinite moment. How does this work? Well, you just need to look at an object in front of you. That's right. You don't have to close your eyes. You don't have to lock yourself away in some sort of private meditation room. You don't have to do any of that. You can be sitting at starbucks and have a coffee cup about a foot or two away from you.

That's all you need. Just focus on an object and block out everything else by actively describing the project to yourself without verbalizing the words. In other words, your 'talking' to yourself with your mind and the dialogue is restricted to the physical description of the object in front of you. Pretty neat, right? Well, the great thing about this is you can achieve a tremendous sense of calm and serenity in a relatively short period of time just by restricting your power of focus to the item in front of you.

Viewing Your Thoughts As Clouds

This is my personal favorite. Using the counting your breath method above, achieve a state of inner calm. You must be in a room where people cannot disturb you. You must devote enough time to this. Maybe 20 minutes per day. You also have to have your eyes closed. Once you achieve a sense of inner calm, you then focus on your thoughts.

Here's the trick. Instead of instantly wanting to explain them analyze them or otherwise get caught up in them, think of your thoughts as clouds. That's right. Clouds form in the sky and they slowly blow away. Treat your thoughts like clouds. Acknowledge that you're thinking them. Acknowledge what they are but do not interpret them. For example, a mental image of my ex-girlfriend flashes in front of me as I meditate. I just acknowledge that that is the image of my ex-girlfriend.

That's the only thing I tell myself or allow myself to be conscious of. I don't dig up the actual fact that she hurt me. I don't focus on the fact that I miss her. Instead, when the image flashes, I just say to myself that is my ex-girlfriend. This way you're not running away from the thought. You're not trying to put it in a can or to control it.

You're not reinterpreting it to be something that it's not. You just acknowledge it. And just like a cloud, it breaks up and then another mental image comes. This is a very powerful technique because it not only delivers personal peace but it helps you become a more disciplined thinker. Just because you get triggered doesn't necessarily mean that you have to lose control. The more you practice this mindfulness technique, you become a stronger individual.

Adopt The Buddy Buddy System

Let's be honest here. You're not the only person dealing with emotional issues. All of us are dealing with some sort of issue. Maybe it takes the form of addiction. Others takes the form of obsession. For others, it takes the form of anger issues. Whatever the case may be, we all have issues. Don't for a second believe that there is such a thing as a perfect human being with absolutely no problems.

More likely than not, if you meet those people, they're probably in denial. At some level or other, they might be sweeping things under the rug and it's only a matter of time until that emotional volcano blows up.

Knowing this, you probably have a friend who is looking to resolve issues as well. Tell that person that you are adopting CBT and if they would like to form an accountability partnership with you.

A buddy buddy system basically means that you give the other person permission to hold you to account. Maybe you would check in with each other once a week and say okay did you guys do this exercises. Did you practice mindfulness at least once every day? Give that person the right to call you into account. In other words, let them know it's perfectly okay if they kick your cage a little bit if you're not sticking to the plan.

They must also give you that same permission. This way you pull each other up. Now, please understand that the buddy buddy system works with somebody that is not your best friend. Seriously, because if you're doing this with your best friend, they love you. They want the best for you. So what will they do? They will indulge. They'll say eventually "It's okay. You don't have to stick to the plan you know. I understand what you're going through and I know. So I want the best for you. So it's ok."

The problem with this is that it's not going to help you. You don't want somebody who will treat you with kid gloves. Instead, you want somebody who will lay down straight. If you stray from the plan, they will let you know. Sometimes, the words hurt. Let it hurt. You have to do whatever it takes to make sure that you stick to the plan because that's how you get better. That's how CBT can turn your life around.

Remember To Celebrate Every Victory... No Matter How Small

Make no mistake. When you adopt CBT, you're actually taking a long journey. This is not something that you are going to pull off overnight. Sure there are some people who respond really well to CBT and they're able to turn their back on addictions, depression, anxiety, mood problems, personality problems, and other issues relatively quickly.

But not everybody's on that same track. Everybody's different. Instead of beating yourself up over the fact that you don't see major changes, focus instead on the small changes that you can see. If you focus enough, you will be able to recognize it. Learn to celebrate them. Seriously, no matter how small these changes are. Celebrate them. Understand that they are achievements. Pat yourself on the back. Allow yourself to feel good about them. As the old saying goes even small steps forward are still steps forward. I wish you nothing but success in your efforts to turn your life around with CBT.

Conclusion

CBT is not a one-size fits all 'magic bullet' solution to all your problems. Depending on the severity of your challenges, CBT might be, at best, a supplemental solution. Still, CBT is a tried and proven framework that has enabled a huge number of people over the years to live more effective and empowered lives. If CBT can help others, it can help you as well.

Do me a big favor. After reading this book, don't just sit on it. Seriously. Don't just settle for the feeling that you CAN do something about your challenges. Feeling good and optimistic can only take you so far. You have to ACT on the information presented in this book. Go through each step.

Please understand that you don't have to quickly zip through each step outlined in this book. Self-help is NOT a race. Instead, fully immerse yourself in the process and allow yourself to be transformed. Maybe it will take you only a couple of days for each step or a few weeks or even months. It doesn't matter. Everyone is different.

What matter is that you are able to fully implement the information contained in this book.

Wishing a life of wellness for you!

Adherence to all applicable laws and regulations, including international, federal, state, and local governing professional licensing, business practices, advertising, and all other aspects of doing business in any jurisdiction in the world is the sole responsibility of the purchaser or reader.

.

Printed in Great Britain
by Amazon